120
300	150
350 (moderate oven)	175
400 (hot oven)	205
450 (very hot oven)	230
500 (extremely hot oven)	260

L E N G T H S

U.S. Measurements	Metric Equivalents
1/4 inch	6 mm
1/2 inch	1.2 cm
3/4 inch	2 cm
1 inch	2.5 cm
2 inches	5 cm
5 inches	12.5 cm

APPLES

APPLES

Andrews McMeel
Publishing

Kansas City

www.andrewsmcmeel.com

ISBN: 0-8362-5228-4

Library of Congress Catalog Card Number: 97-74513

First U.S. Edition

1 2 3 4 5 6 7 8 9 10

Editor: Deborah Mintcheff
Designer: Yolanda Monteza
Photographer: Steven Mark Needham
Illustrator: Ed Lam

**Produced by
Smallwood & Stewart, Inc.,
New York City**

TABLE OF CONTENTS

A P P L

Have you had a bite of the forbidden fruit recently or sampled from the tree of knowledge? If you have, you're not alone. The average American consumes about eighteen pounds of apples each year. This means that we snack on approximately 55 percent of the U.S. apple crop.

Throughout history, apples have played a part in superstition, mythology, folklore, and religion. They have been the subject of choice for the world's great

E S 🍏

still-life painters, and have been given to favorite teachers by children for decades.

Where the first uncultivated apples grew is in dispute. Some experts believe that the apple originated in Southeast Asia, while others believe it was nearer to the Baltic Sea. We do know, however, that the Egyptians grew apples as far back as the thirteenth century B.C.

Today, there are over eight thousand apple varieties cultivated in countries including France, Russia, China, and the United States. Here, the top-producing states are Washington, Pennsylvania, California, Michigan, and New York, but apples are grown in every state except Hawaii and Alaska. More than two thousand varieties are grown in U.S. orchards, but approximately a dozen varieties are grown commercially, and supermarkets only stock apples from that dozen.

It is interesting that the number-one selling apple in the United States is the

Red Delicious, though it is far from the tastiest apple available. It is, however, an apple growers' dream—bright red, well-shaped, well-recognized, available year round, and hardy enough to withstand long-distance transportation.

Here, we had the difficult task of choosing only twelve apple varieties to discuss. Some will be familiar to you, and others that are less familiar are destined to become new favorites with your family and in your kitchen.

APPLE NUTRITION

An apple a day may or may not keep the doctor away, but it is a fact that apples are nutritious as well as delicious.

A medium apple (about 5 ounces):
- contains 80 calories
- is cholesterol-, fat- and sodium-free
- contains 5 grams of fiber
- is a source of vitamins A and C, as well as potassium

Buying and Storing Apples

Take the time to find the best-quality apples in your area. When possible, buy them at roadside stands and at farmers' markets, where you will find apples picked at their peak of flavor. Look for well-shaped, firm, brightly colored fruit that is heavy for its size and free of any bruises. When possible, purchase fruit that has not been waxed. It's easy to tell—waxed fruit is unnaturally shiny. When buying apples, keep in mind that larger apples ripen faster than smaller ones. Store apples in the crisper drawer of the refrigerator or in a covered container.

APPLES AT

VARIETY	TEXTURE/FLAVOR
Cortland	semi-firm/tart-sweet
Empire	crisp & juicy/slightly tart
Golden Delicious	firm & juicy/sweet
Granny Smith	firm/tart-sweet
Idared	semi-firm & juicy/sweet
Jonagold	firm & crisp/tart-sweet
McIntosh	firm & juicy/sweet & flavorful
Macoun	crisp & fine textured/tart-sweet
Mutsu	crisp & juicy/spicy & sweet
Northern Spy	firm/tart-sweet
Rome	firm/slightly sweet
Winesap	crisp & juicy/rich winey flavor

A GLANCE

AVAILABILITY	BEST USES
Sept. to spring	pies, all-purpose
Sept. to spring	all-purpose
Year round	eating, all-purpose
Year round	eating, all-purpose
Sept. to early spring	eating, pies, all-purpose
Late Sept. to Oct.	eating, all-purpose
Sept. to early summer	eating, good for most cooking
Sept. to early spring	eating, salads, pies, cooking
Sept. to June	eating, salads, applesauce
Oct. to Dec.	pies, cakes, applesauce
Oct. to July	all-purpose
Sept. to spring	applesauce, pies, cider

TYPES OF APPLES

CORTLAND: This fine-textured, good-flavored red apple is grown mainly in the Northeast. The Cortland is a cross between the McIntosh and the Ben Davis. It has thin skin and very juicy, white flesh that is pleasantly tart. The Cortland makes a great everyday apple since it is well suited for most purposes. Its flesh stays white longer than other varieties, making it ideal for salads. Cortlands are also excellent for applesauce and baking.

EMPIRE: The Empire is a cross between the Red Delicious and McIntosh apples. Its bright color, tangy flavor, and keeping qualities make it popular among growers. It resembles the McIntosh in shape, but its skin is covered with the white specks we have come to associate with Red Delicious apples. Its flesh is creamy white, juicy, and crisp. The Empire is sweet enough for eating out of hand and is also good for salads, applesauce, and cooking.

GOLDEN DELICIOUS: This tasty gold-colored apple is easy to like and always available. It has thin skin and semi-firm, crisp flesh that is flavorful and juicy. Golden Delicious apples are as tasty raw as they are in cakes, applesauce, and pies. It is the apple of choice for the classic French dessert Tarte Tatin as the Golden Delicious holds its shape exceptionally well. For the best flavor, choose apples that are greenish yellow or deep golden in color.

GRANNY SMITH: It took a long time for the Australian Granny Smith apple to gain popularity in the United States: Americans thought green apples were suitable only for baking. But once these apples caught on, they soared in popularity. The Granny Smith's generous size and tart-sweet flavor have contributed to its success. It is a great all-purpose apple—good for cakes, pies, stuffing, juice, and for simply snacking.

IDARED: The brilliant lipstick-red skin of the Idared gives little indication of what lies below: a pale yellow, juicy, fine-textured flesh whose perfume is particularly enticing. Developed in the early 1940s, Idareds are grown primarily in the East and Midwest. They are harvested from the end of September through October. Idareds hold their shape especially well in pies, and they make a luscious pink-hued applesauce when their skin is left on.

JONAGOLD: In 1968, a cross between the Jonathan and Golden Delicious apples produced the Jonagold, which inherited the perfume of the Golden Delicious and the bright tart-sweet flavor of the Jonathan. It is distinguished from its parents by its striking yellow-and-red color. Its flavorful flesh is crisp and creamy yellow. Jonagolds are picked in September and October, and they are favored for pies and applesauce.

McINTOSH: First introduced in the late nineteenth century, the McIntosh eventually became parent to the Empire, Cortland, Macoun, and Spartan apples. Being too soft to hold up well to baking, it is used mainly for eating, apple cider, and applesauce. It has very white, tender flesh and an aroma reminiscent of familiar winter spices. The McIntosh is cultivated in most of the apple-growing areas throughout the United States.

MACOUN: Pronounced ma-COON, this is a cross between the ever-popular McIntosh and the Jersey Black apple. Anyone who has journeyed to Upstate New York in the fall will recall seeing Macouns at roadside stands. This apple tastes best when freshly picked. The Macoun has white flesh that is fragrant, juicy, and firm, making it a great pie apple as well as a tasty snack. If you can't find Macouns in your area, Empires are a good substitute.

MUTSU: This apple is also known by the name Crispin. It has crisp, sweet, white flesh with just a slight hint of tartness. The Mutsu is a great cider apple and is a good choice for country-style desserts such as crisps, cobblers, and grunts. Mutsus are available almost all year round. When purchasing Mutsus, avoid any with a greenish cast—they were picked before reaching their peak of flavor.

NORTHERN SPY: Many pie aficionados believe that this is the only pie apple and it is easy to see why. A pie made with Northern Spys will be juicy, with rich complex flavors that are a perfect balance of sweet and tart. Northern Spys are also excellent baked, eaten out of hand, in salads, dried, and canned. Grown primarily in New York and Michigan, Northern Spys are harvested in the fall and are available from the late fall into the early winter.

ROME: This apple is also known by the name Rome Beauty. Romes are readily available in supermarkets from late October until July, but its peak of flavor lasts only through October. The Rome has a deep red color and a generous round shape. This apple tastes delicious baked whole, in cider, or as an addition to most salads. The Rome's greenish white flesh is firm with a pleasant slightly sweet flavor.

WINESAP: The Winesap has a bold, heady bouquet that is unmistakable. Its skin is burgundy and its firm, yellow flesh is syrupy with red cherry and wine undertones. The Winesap's complex flavor makes it ideal for all sorts of baked goods and cider. Growers harvest this apple from late September to early November, and it can be purchased well into the early spring. The Stayman Winesap, a cousin of the Winesap, has a milder taste and greenish yellow flesh.

R E C I

PES

Butternut Squash and Apple Soup with Parmesan Croutons

Roasting apples caramelizes their natural sugars and lends this soup an especially luscious flavor. It would be the perfect first course for a roasted chicken, turkey, or pork dinner.

Parmesan Croutons

3 cups cubed ($1/2$-inch) French bread

3 tablespoons freshly grated
    Parmesan cheese

2 tablespoons olive oil

$3^{1}/_{2}$ pounds butternut squash, peeled,
    seeded, and cut into chunks
    (about 4 cups)

2 large red apples, peeled, cored,
    and cut into chunks

3 tablespoons butter

$1/2$ cup chopped onions

1 garlic clove, minced

6 cups chicken broth

$1/4$ cup dry sherry

Salt and freshly ground pepper

Prepare the Parmesan croutons: Preheat the oven to 350°F. In a medium bowl, toss the bread cubes with the Parmesan and oil. Spread the croutons in a single layer on a baking sheet and bake, tossing occasionally, for 12 minutes, or until golden brown. Set aside.

Increase the oven temperature to 375°F. Place the squash and apples on a baking sheet and roast, stirring, for 30 minutes, or until tender.

In a large pot, melt the butter over medium heat. Add the onions and garlic; cook for 3 to 5 minutes, until the onions are softened. Stir in the squash and apples, the broth, sherry, $1/2$ teaspoon salt, and $1/4$ teaspoon pepper. Bring to a boil, then reduce the heat and simmer for 15 minutes or until the flavors of the soup have fully developed.

In a blender or food processor, puree the soup, working in batches if necessary. Return the soup to the pot, season to taste with salt and pepper if necessary, and reheat.

To serve, ladle the soup into bowls and top with the Parmesan croutons. *Serves 6*

Sauteed Apple Rings

Core 2 large red apples such as Empire or McIntosh and cut into $1/2$-inch-thick slices. In a large heavy skillet, melt 3 tablespoons unsalted butter over medium-high heat. Add half the apple slices and sprinkle with sugar. Cook for 3 minutes, or until golden. Turn the apples and sprinkle them with more sugar. Continue cooking, adding additional butter if needed, for 3 minutes longer, or until golden. Transfer the apple slices to a platter, cover, and cook the remaining apple slices. Serve with pork chops or roasted chicken. *Serves 4*

Brown-Sugar Baked Apples

Preheat the oven to 375°F. Core large baking apples such as McIntosh or Cortland to within $1/2$ inch of the bottom. Sprinkle the cavities with ground cinnamon, fill with brown sugar, and squeeze fresh lemon juice over the tops. Place a bit of unsalted butter on top of each apple and put the apples into a shallow baking dish. Add enough hot water to just cover the bottom of the baking dish. Bake the apples for 35 to 45 minutes, until tender when pierced with a wooden pick, adding additional water to the baking dish if needed. Serve the baked apples warm or cold, accompanied by vanilla ice cream.

Baby Spinach Salad with Curry Dressing

Tart green apples, dried apricots, almonds, and tender spinach leaves combine for a salad that strikes the perfect balance of color, texture, and flavor. For lunch, serve this with thick slices of crusty sourdough bread.

Curry Dressing
1 small garlic clove, minced
1 teaspoon minced peeled fresh ginger
1 teaspoon curry powder
$3/4$ teaspoon sugar
$1/4$ teaspoon salt
Freshly ground pepper
$1/4$ cup dry white wine
$1^1/2$ tablespoons white vinegar
$1/2$ cup olive oil

2 medium green apples, cored
        and cut into $1/2$-inch chunks
$1/4$ cup snipped dried apricots
1 pound baby spinach, washed
$1/2$ cup sliced almonds, toasted

Prepare the curry dressing: In a blender, combine the garlic, ginger, curry powder, sugar, salt, pepper to taste, wine, and vinegar; process until blended. With the machine running, add the oil in a slow stream, processing until smooth. Transfer the dressing to a medium bowl.

Add the apples and apricots, tossing until coated. Let stand at room temperature for about 30 minutes to allow the flavors to blend. Put the spinach leaves into a serving bowl. Add the dressing and fruit mixture, tossing until well mixed. Sprinkle with the almonds and serve.

Serves 4 to 6

Goat Cheese Salad with Hazelnut Vinaigrette

Fresh goat cheese, also known as chèvre, has a delicate tangy flavor. Here, it is baked just long enough to give it a meltingly creamy texture that contrasts beautifully with the crisp salad greens and the sweet apple.

1 (6-ounce) log fresh goat cheese
1/2 cup hazelnuts, toasted and chopped*

Hazelnut Vinaigrette
2 tablespoons extra-virgin olive oil
1 tablespoon hazelnut oil
1 tablespoon tarragon vinegar
Salt and freshly ground pepper

8 cups mixed salad greens, such as
     baby red or green leaf lettuce,
     arugula, radicchio, or endive
1 large Golden Delicious apple, halved,
     cored, and thinly sliced

*Put the hazelnuts into a baking pan in a
  375°F oven for about 8 minutes, or until
  golden; rub the skins off with a towel.

Preheat the oven to 400°F. Cut the goat cheese into 6 rounds and coat them completely with the nuts. Transfer the cheese to a small baking sheet and refrigerate.

Prepare the hazelnut vinaigrette: In a small bowl, whisk together the olive and hazelnut oils and the vinegar. Season to taste with salt and pepper. Put the greens and apple into a large bowl and drizzle with the dressing, tossing until coated. Arrange on serving plates; set aside.

Bake the cheese rounds for about 5 minutes, or until warmed through but not melting. Using a metal spatula, place a cheese round on top of each salad. Serve immediately. *Serves 6*

Apple-Oat Crisp

Preheat the oven to 350°F. Put 3 Granny Smith apples, peeled, cored, and sliced, into a deep-dish pie plate or other baking dish. In a medium bowl, combine 2 cups rolled oats, $^1/_2$ cup packed brown sugar, $^1/_2$ cup chopped walnuts, $^1/_2$ cup raisins, $^1/_2$ teaspoon ground cinnamon, a pinch of freshly grated nutmeg, and 1 teaspoon vanilla. Using your fingers, blend in $^1/_2$ cup (1 stick) unsalted butter, cut into bits, until the mixture resembles coarse meal. Sprinkle over the apples. Bake the crisp for 30 minutes, or until golden brown on top. *Serves 6*

Apple and Napa Cabbage Slaw

Apple cider vinegar, celery seeds, and a touch of sugar give this colorful salad a taste reminiscent of old-fashioned coleslaw dressing. The napa cabbage stays nicely crisp and its mild flavor is a good balance for the apples.

1 red and 1 green apple, halved,
     cored, and thinly sliced
3 tablespoons fresh lemon juice
1 1/2 cups finely shredded napa cabbage
1/2 cup diced celery
2 tablespoons chopped fresh parsley
1 tablespoon snipped fresh chives

Cider Vinegar Dressing
3 tablespoons apple cider vinegar
1 teaspoon Dijon mustard
1/2 teaspoon celery seeds
1/2 teaspoon sugar
1/4 teaspoon salt
1/4 teaspoon freshly ground pepper
Pinch of ground red pepper
1/3 cup olive oil

In a large bowl, toss the apples with the lemon juice until well coated. Add the cabbage, celery, parsley, and chives, tossing until well combined.

Prepare the cider vinegar dressing: In a small bowl, whisk together the vinegar, mustard, celery seeds, sugar, salt, and both peppers until smooth. Add the oil in a slow, steady stream, whisking until blended. Pour the dressing over the slaw, tossing until the vegetables are evenly coated. Cover and marinate in the refrigerator for at least 30 minutes or up to several hours before serving. *Serves 4 to 6*

Pink Applesauce

Select just a single type or a variety of red cooking apples. Wash the apples and cut into large chunks. Pour about $1/4$ inch of cold water into a nonreactive saucepan and add the apples. Cook the apples over medium heat, stirring often, until the apples are very soft and falling apart. Remove from the heat and add sugar to taste, stirring until it is dissolved. If desired, add a little fresh lemon juice or a pinch of ground cinnamon or grated nutmeg. Strain the applesauce through a food mill. Serve warm or chilled.

Apple, Rye Bread, and Sausage Stuffing

Rye bread with caraway seeds is an ideal match for the sweet apples, sausage, and aromatic fresh sage in this robust stuffing. It makes a tempting side dish as well as a delicious stuffing for chicken or duck.

$^1/_2$ **pound sweet Italian sausage,**
  casings removed

2 tablespoons olive or vegetable oil

$^1/_3$ **cup chopped onion**

$^1/_3$ **cup chopped celery**

$2^1/_2$ **cups cubed ($^1/_2$-inch) day-old**
  rye bread

1 large red apple, cored and chopped

$^1/_2$ **cup raisins**

$^1/_4$ **cup chopped fresh flat-leaf parsley**

1 teaspoon dried sage

$^1/_2$ **teaspoon salt**

$^1/_2$ **teaspoon freshly ground pepper**

$^1/_2$ **cup chicken broth or water**

$^1/_4$ **cup ($^1/_2$ stick) butter, melted**

Preheat the oven to 375°F.

In a small skillet, cook the sausage over medium heat, breaking it up, for 6 minutes, or until well browned and cooked through. Using a slotted spoon, transfer the sausage to a large bowl and set aside. Wipe out the skillet.

Add the oil to the skillet and heat over medium heat. Add the onion and celery and cook, stirring, for 4 minutes, or until the onion is softened. Off heat, add the sausage, bread cubes, apple, raisins, parsley, sage, salt, and pepper. Pour the broth over and toss until mixed. Spoon the stuffing into a shallow baking dish and drizzle with the melted butter. Bake for 30 minutes, or until golden brown on top. *Serves 4 to 6*

Baked-Apple-and-
Sweet-Potato Puree

Preheat the oven to 375°F. Place 3 large sweet potatoes and 3 large Granny Smith apples on a baking sheet. Prick them with a fork in several places. Bake the potatoes for about 1 hour, or until soft. Bake the apples for about 45 minutes, or until soft. Remove from the oven and cool slightly. Peel the sweet potatoes and pass through a food mill set over a large bowl. Cut the apples into large chunks and pass through the food mill. Stir in $1/2$ teaspoon ground cinnamon and season with salt and pepper. *Serves 6*

Skillet Apple Pancake

There are countless versions of this classic German skillet pancake. Here, the traditionally thin pancake is topped with a mantle of caramelized Granny Smith apples, which adds just the right amount of sweetness.

$^1/_2$ cup all-purpose flour

$^1/_2$ cup milk

3 large eggs

2 medium Granny Smith apples,
    peeled, halved, cored, and
    cut into $^1/_4$-inch-thick slices

$^1/_4$ cup sugar

$^1/_4$ teaspoon ground cinnamon

$^1/_4$ cup ($^1/_2$ stick) unsalted butter

Preheat the oven to 375°F.

Put the flour into a medium bowl. In a small bowl, whisk together the milk and eggs. Pour the milk mixture over the flour, gently whisking just until blended. Set aside.

In a medium bowl, toss the apples with 3 tablespoons of the sugar and the cinnamon until the apples are evenly coated.

In a large cast-iron or heavy ovenproof non-stick skillet, melt 3 tablespoons of the butter over medium-high heat. Carefully tilt the pan to coat the bottom and sides evenly with the butter. Place the apple slices in an even layer in the skillet. Cook, shaking the pan, for 5 minutes, or until the apples are softened and the sugar has begun to turn golden brown. Pour the batter evenly over the apples.

Place the skillet in the oven and bake for 18 to 20 minutes, until the pancake is completely set. Using a narrow spatula, carefully loosen the pancake from the sides of the skillet.

Place a plate on top of the pancake and invert. Slide the pancake back into the skillet, dot with the remaining 1 tablespoon butter, and sprinkle with the remaining 1 tablespoon sugar. Return the skillet to the oven for 5 minutes, or until the sugar has caramelized. Cut the pancake into wedges and serve. *Serves 4*

Green Apple Sorbet

In a blender or food processor, combine 6 medium Granny Smith apples, peeled, cored, and coarsely chopped, with $1/2$ cup superfine sugar, and $1/4$ cup fresh lemon juice. Process the mixture until it is smooth.

Transfer the puree to an ice-cream maker and freeze according to the manufacturer's instructions. Spoon into an air-tight container and store in the freezer for up to 4 days. *Serves 6*

Pork Medallions
with Apple Cider Sauce

Using a combination of fresh apples and cider intensifies the apple flavor of the sauce, making this a tempting main course for a casual fall dinner with family or friends.

Apple Cider Sauce

3 medium red apples, peeled,
    halved, cored, and cut
    into $1/2$-inch cubes

2 shallots, finely chopped

3 small gherkins, thinly sliced

$1/2$ cup apple cider or apple juice

$1/2$ cup heavy cream

1 tablespoon apple cider vinegar

1 tablespoon Dijon mustard

$1/4$ teaspoon salt

$1/4$ teaspoon freshly ground pepper

1 tablespoon butter, or more if needed

1 tablespoon olive oil, or more if needed

$1^1/2$ pounds pork tenderloin, cut into
    $3/4$-inch-thick slices

Salt and freshly ground pepper

Prepare the Apple Cider Sauce: In a medium bowl, combine all the ingredients. Set aside.

In a large skillet, heat the butter and oil over medium heat. Season the pork with salt and pepper. Cook for 4 minutes on each side, or until almost cooked through. Transfer the pork to a plate, cover, and set aside.

Pour the sauce ingredients into the skillet. Cook over medium-high heat, stirring, for 10 minutes, or until the sauce has reduced and the apples are tender. Return the pork to the skillet, reduce the heat to medium-low, and cook until the pork is heated through. Transfer the pork and the sauce to a platter and serve. *Serves 4*

The Best-Ever Apple Pie

Whether you like apples that hold their shape or go soft, or a sweet or green apple flavor, choosing the "right" pie apple is a matter of personal taste. For the best varieties, buy your apples at a farmers' market.

2¹/₂ pounds apples, peeled, halved,
        cored, and cut into ¹/₂-inch-thick
        slices (about 6 cups)

Juice of ¹/₂ lemon

³/₄ cup sugar

3 tablespoons all-purpose flour

1 teaspoon ground cinnamon

¹/₄ teaspoon freshly grated nutmeg

Dough for 9-inch double-crust pie,
        divided in half

2 tablespoons unsalted butter,
        cut into bits

Preheat the oven to 425°F.

In a large bowl, toss the apples with the lemon juice. Add the sugar, flour, cinnamon, and nutmeg, tossing until the apples are coated. Set the mixture aside.

On a lightly floured surface, roll out one piece of the dough into a ¹/₈-inch-thick round and fit into a 9-inch pie plate. Spoon in the apple filling and dot with the butter. Roll out the remaining dough and drape over the filling. Trim and crimp the edges. Cut several steam vents in the top.

Bake the pie for 15 minutes. Reduce the heat to 375°F and bake for 30 minutes longer, or until the pastry is browned and the filling is bubbling. Place on a wire rack to cool. *Serves 8*

French Apple Tart

This simple tart is ideal when friends stop by. The dough can be prepared ahead and refrigerated or frozen, and the custard filling and apple topping are no fuss at all. Serve this tart warm or at room temperature.

Dough for 9-inch single-crust pie

**3 large Granny Smith apples, peeled,
halved, cored, and thinly sliced**

$1/2$ cup sugar

$1/2$ cup heavy cream

1 large egg

1 teaspoon vanilla extract

Confectioners' sugar for sprinkling

Preheat the oven to 375°F.

On a lightly floured surface, roll the dough into a $^1/_8$-inch-thick round. Transfer the dough to a 9-inch tart pan with a removable bottom and press into the pan. Trim the overhanging dough.

Arrange the apple slices in slightly overlapping circles. Bake for 15 minutes.

Meanwhile, in a small bowl, whisk together the sugar, cream, egg, and vanilla. Pour over the apples and bake the tart for 25 minutes longer, or until the custard is set. Cool the tart on a wire rack for 10 minutes. Remove the sides of the pan and sprinkle the tart with confectioners' sugar. *Serves 8*

Picking Your Own Apples

Picking your own is the best way to ensure that you are getting apples at their ripest and freshest. You can also make some great discoveries, since these orchards grow the harder-to-find old-fashioned varieties. Each fall in the apple-growing areas, local newspapers do a roundup of the many pick-your-own-orchards. And many state agricultural departments publish guides to orchards. Taking a drive into the country on a crisp autumn day to pick apples is fun, especially when topped off with a picnic lunch.

LIQUID MEASURES

Spoons and Cups		Metric Equivalents
½ tsp.		2.5 ml
1 tsp.		5 ml
1 Tbs. (3 tsp.)		15 ml
¼ cup		60 ml
⅓ cup	(tsp.: teaspoon/Tbs.: tablespoon)	80 ml
½ cup		120 ml
1 cup (8 ounces)		240 ml
4 cups (1 quart)		950 ml
4 quarts (1 gallon)		3.8 liters

WEIGHTS

Ounces and Pounds	Metric Equivalents
½ ounce	14 g
1 ounce	28 g
2 ounces	57 g
4 ounces (¼ pound)	113 g
8 ounces (½ pound)	225 g
16 ounces (1 pound)	454 g

A Robert Frederick Miniature • A Robert Frederick Miniature •
A Robert Frederick Miniature • A Robert Frederick Miniature • A Robert Frederick Miniature •
A Robert Frederick Miniature • A Robert Frederick Miniature • A Robert Frederick
A Robert Frederick Miniature • A Robert Frederick Miniature • A Robert Frederick Miniature •
A Robert Frederick Miniature • A Robert Frederick Miniature • A Robert Frederick
A Robert Frederick Miniature • A Robert Frederick Miniature • A Robert Frederick Miniature •
A Robert Frederick Miniature • A Robert Frederick Miniature • A Robert
A Robert Frederick Miniature • A Robert Frederick Miniature • A Robert Frederick Miniature •
A Robert Frederick Miniature • A Robert Frederick Miniature • A Robert Frederick
A Robert Frederick Miniature • A Robert Frederick Miniature • A Robert Frederick Miniature •
A Robert Frederick Miniature • A Robert Frederick Miniature • A Robert
A Robert Frederick Miniature • A Robert Frederick Miniature • A Robert Frederick Miniature •
A Robert Frederick Miniature • A Robert Frederick Miniature • A Robert Frederick
A Robert Frederick Miniature • A Robert Frederick Miniature • A Robert Frederick Miniature •
A Robert Frederick Miniature • A Robert Frederick Miniature • A Robert
A Robert Frederick Miniature • A Robert Frederick Miniature • A Robert Frederick Miniature •
A Robert Frederick Miniature • A Robert Frederick Miniature • A Robert
A Robert Frederick Miniature • A Robert Frederick Miniature • A Robert Frederick Miniature •
A Robert Frederick Miniature • A Robert Frederick Miniature • A Robert Frederick
A Robert Frederick Miniature • A Robert Frederick Miniature • A Robert Frederick Miniature •
A Robert Frederick Miniature • A Robert Frederick Miniature • A Robert Frederick
A Robert Frederick Miniature • A Robert Frederick Miniature • A Robert Frederick Miniature •
A Robert Frederick Miniature • A Robert Frederick Miniature • A Robert Frederick
A Robert Frederick Miniature • A Robert Frederick Miniature • A Robert Frederick Miniature •

This edition copyright © Robert Frederick Ltd.
Downwood, Claverton Down Road, Bath BA2 6DT

First Published 1993

Acknowledgments
Typesetting: Creative Design and Typesetting
Printed in the UK

Disclaimer
While every effort has been made to ensure the accuracy of the
information contained herein, the Publishers do not hold them-
selves responsible for any inaccuracy.

Travel
Records

A Robert Frederick Miniature

Personal Details

Name ....

Address ....

Telephone : Home ....

               Business ....

               Car ....

Useful Information

Nat. Insurance No. ....

Passport No. ....

Driving Licence No. ....

Car Key No. ....

Car Insurance Pol. No. ....

Renewal Date ....

Motor Club M'ship No. ....

Credit Card Nos. ....

....

In Case of Emergency

Contact ....

Address ....

....

....

Tel. No. ....

Blood Group ....

Known Allergies ....

....

....

Notes

....

....

....

....

Metric Conversions

Length

1 centimetre (cm)		= 0.3937 in
1 metre (m)	= 100 cm	= 1.0936 yds
1 kilometre (km)	= 1000 m	= 0,6214 mile
1 inch		= 2.5400 cm
1 yard	= 36 in	= 0.9144 m
1 mile	= 1760 yds	= 1.6093 km

Capacity

1 cu dm (dm3)	= 1000 cm³	= 0.0353 cu ft
1 cu metre (m3)	= 1000 dm³	= 1.3080 cu yds
1 litre	= 1dm³	= 0.2200 gallon
1 cu yd	= 27 cu ft	= 0.7646 m³
1 pint	= 4 gills	= 0.5683 litre
1 gallon	= 8 pints	= 4.5461 litres

Weight

1 gramme (g)	= 1000 mg	= 0.3535 oz
1 kilogramme (kg)	= 1000 g	= 2.2046 lb
1 tonne (t)	= 1000 kg	= 0.9842 ton
1 ounce	= 437.5 grains	= 28.350 g
1 pound	= 16 oz	= 0.4536 kg
1 ton	= 2240 pounds	= 1.0161 tonnes

Area

1 sq metre (m2)	= 10 000 cm²	= 1.1960 sq yds
1 hectare (ha)	= 10 000 m²	= 2.4711 acres
1 sq km (km2)	= 100 hectares	= 0.3861 sq mile
1 sq yd	= 9 sq ft	= 0.8361m²
1 acre	= 4840 sq yds	= 4046.9m²

Metric Conversions

Metric Conversions	multiply by
acres to hectares	0.4047
cubic inches to cubic centimetres	16.39
cubic feet to cubic metres	0.02832
cubic yards to cubic metres	0.7646
cubic inches to litres	0.01639
feet to metres	0.3048
gallons to litres	4.546
grains to grammes	0.0648
inches to centimetres	2.540
miles to kilometres	1.609
ounces to grammes	28.35
pounds to kilogrammes	0.4536
pounds to grammes	453.6
square inches to square centimetres	6.452
square feet to square metres	0.0929
square yards to square metres	0.8361
square miles to square kilometres	2.590
tons to kilogrammes	1016.00
yards to metres	0.9144

International Information

Country	Capital	Air Distance /London	GMT	Dial Codes From	To
Australia	Canberra	10563	+10	0011	61
Austria	Vienna	790	+1	00	43
Belgium	Brussels	217	+1	00	32
Canada	Ottawa	3321	-5	011	1
Denmark	Copenhagen	608	+1	009	45
Finland	Helsinki	1147	+2	990	358
France	Paris	215	+1	19	33
Germany	Bonn (Berlin)	320	+1	00	49
Hong Kong	Victoria	5990	+8	106	852
Hungary	Budapest	923	+1	00	36
India	New Delhi	4180	+5.5	900	91
Ireland (Rep) *	Dublin	279	GMT	16	353
Italy	Rome	895	+1	00	39
Japan	Tokyo	5956	+9	001	81

International Information

Country	Capital	Air Distance /London	GMT	Dial Codes From	To
Luxembourg	Luxembourg	310	+1	00	352
Malta	Valletta	1305	+1	0	356
Netherlands	Amsterdam	230	+1	09	31
New Zealand	Wellington	11692	+12	00	64
Norway	Oslo	723	+1	095	47
Pakistan	Islamabad	3767	+5	00	92
Poland	Warsaw	912	+1	00	48
Portugal	Lisbon	972	GMT	07	351
Spain	Madrid	773	+1	07	34
Sweden	Stockholm	908	+1	009	46
Switzerland	Berne	476	+1	00	41
USA	Washington DC	3665	-5	011	1
USSR	Moscow	1557	+3	810	7
Yugoslavia	Belgrade	1056	+1	99	38

U.K. Dial Codes : From 010, To 44

Travel Records

Trip 1

*Every perfect traveller always creates the
country where he travels.*

Nikos Kazantzakis

Travel Records

Where Visited ....

....

Date of Departure ....

Date of Return ....

Who Went ....

....

....

....

....

....

Mode(s) of
Transport
☐ Car   ☐ Plane   ☐ Boat

☐ Train   ☐ Other ....

Accommodation
☐ Hotel   ☐ B&B/ Guest Hs.   ☐ With friends/ Self-catering

☐ Camping/ Caravan   ☐ Other ....

Travel Records

Packing List

....
....
....
....
....
....
....
....
....
....
....
....
....
....
....
....

He who would travel happily must travel light.
Saint-Exupéry

Travel Records

Packing List (cont.)

....

....

....

....

....

....

Check List (before leaving home)
e.g. turning off taps, locking doors & windows etc.

....

....

....

....

....

Travel Records

Expenses

Budget ....

Foreign Currency ....

Travellers Cheques (or similar) ....

Major Expenditure Item	*Amount*	
	Allocated	Spent
Travel		
Accommodation		
Dining Out		
Sight Seeing		
Souvenirs & Gifts		
Clothes		
First Aid		

Travel Records

Insurance Details

....

....

Travel Agent Details

....

Important Numbers

....

....

....

....

....

Notes

....

....

....

Travel Records

Diary

(using this format you can write as little or as much about each day as you like)

Date   Description

....
....
....
....
....
....
....
....
....
....
....
....
....

Travel Records

Diary

Date   Description

....

....

....

....

....

....

....

....

....

....

....

....

Travel Records

Diary

Date   Description

....

....

....

....

....

....

....

....

....

....

....

....

Travel Records

Diary

Date   Description

....

....

....

....

....

....

....

....

....

....

....

....

Travel Records

Diary

Date	Description
	....
	....
	....
	....
	....
	....
	....
	....
	....
	....
	....
	....
	....

Travel Records

Special Memories

Favourite Excursion:

....

....

....

....

....

....

Favourite Meal:

....

....

....

....

Travel Records

Special Memories (Cont.)

Favourite Place:

....

....

....

....

....

....

Notes:

....

....

....

....

Travel Records

Souvenirs

Item   Where Bought

....

....

....

....

Gifts

Item   For Whom

....

....

....

....

....

Travel Records

Trip 2

*Travel is ninety per cent anticipation and
ten per cent recollection.*

Edward Streeter

Travel Records

Where Visited ....

Date of Departure ....

Date of Return ....

Who Went ....

....

....

....

....

....

....

Mode(s) of Transport

- [ ] Car
- [ ] Plane
- [ ] Boat
- [ ] Train
- [ ] Other ....

Accommodation

- [ ] Hotel
- [ ] B&B/ Guest Hs.
- [ ] With friends/ Self-catering
- [ ] Camping/ Caravan
- [ ] Other ....

Travel Records

Packing List

....
....
....
....
....
....
....
....
....
....
....
....

Travel Records

Packing List (cont.)

....

....

....

....

....

....

Check List (before leaving home)
e.g. turning off taps, locking doors & windows etc.

....

....

....

....

....

Travel Records

Expenses

Budget ....

Foreign Currency ....

Travellers Cheques (or similar) ....

Major Expenditure Item	Amount	
	Allocated	Spent
Travel		
Accommodation		
Dining Out		
Sight Seeing		
Souvenirs & Gifts		
Clothes		
First Aid		

Travel Records

Insurance Details

....

....

Travel Agent Details

....

Important Numbers

....

....

....

....

....

Notes

....

....

....

Travel Records

Diary

(using this format you can write as little or as much about each day as you like)

Date | Description

....

....

....

....

....

....

....

....

....

....

....

....

....

....

Travel Records

Diary

Date   Description

....

....

....

....

....

....

....

....

....

....

....

Travel Records

Diary

Date   Description

....
....
....
....
....
....
....
....
....
....
....
....
....
....
....
....
....
....

Travel Records

Diary

Date   Description

....

....

....

....

....

....

....

....

....

....

....

....

Travel Records

Diary

Date   Description

....

....

....

....

....

....

....

....

....

....

....

....

Travel Records

Special Memories

Favourite Excursion:

....

....

....

....

....

....

Favourite Meal:

....

....

....

....

Travel Records

Special Memories (Cont.)

Favourite Place:

....

....

....

....

....

....

Notes:

....

....

....

....

....

Travel Records

Souvenirs

Item   Where Bought

....

....

....

....

....

Gifts

Item   For Whom

....

....

....

....

....

....

Travel Records

Trip 3

Travel is fatal to prejudice, bigotry and narrow-mindedness

Mark Twain

Travel Records

Where Visited ....

Date of Departure ....

Date of Return ....

Who Went ....

....

....

....

....

....

Mode(s) of Transport

☐ Car ☐ Plane ☐ Boat

☐ Train ☐ Other ....

Accommodation

☐ Hotel ☐ B&B/ Guest Hs. ☐ With friends/ Self-catering

☐ Camping/ Caravan ☐ Other ....

Travel Records

Packing List

....
....
....
....
....
....
....
....
....
....
....
....
....
....

Travel Records

Packing List (cont.)

.... | ....

.... | ....

.... | ....

.... | ....

.... | ....

Check List (before leaving home)
e.g. turning off taps, locking doors & windows etc.

.... | ....

.... | ....

.... | ....

.... | ....

.... | ....

Travel Records

Expenses

Budget ....

Foreign Currency ....

Travellers Cheques (or similar) ....

| Major Expenditure | Amount | |
Item	Allocated	Spent
Travel		
Accommodation		
Dining Out		
Sight Seeing		
Souvenirs & Gifts		
Clothes		
First Aid		
.		

Travel Records

Insurance Details

....

....

Travel Agent Details

....

Important Numbers

....

....

....

....

....

....

Notes

....

....

....

Travel Records

Diary

(using this format you can write as little or as much about each day as you like)

Date   Description

....

....

....

....

....

....

....

....

....

....

....

....

....

Travel Records

Diary

Date   Description

....

....

....

....

....

....

....

....

....

....

....

....

Travel Records

Diary

Date   Description

....
....
....
....
....
....
....
....
....
....
....
....
....
....
....
....
....

Travel Records

Diary

Date   Description

....

....

....

....

....

....

....

....

....

....

....

....

....

....

Travel Records

Diary

Date   Description

....

....

....

....

....

....

....

....

....

....

....

....

....

Travel Records

Special Memories

Favourite Excursion:

....

....

....

....

....

....

....

Favourite Meal:

....

....

....

....

Travel Records

Special Memories (Cont.)

Favourite Place:

....

....

....

....

....

....

Notes:

....

....

....

....

....

Travel Records

Souvenirs

Item	Where Bought
....	....
....	....
....	....
....	....

Gifts

Item	For Whom
....	....
....	....
....	....
....	....
....	....

Travel Records

Trip 4

*A man must carry knowledge with him if
he would bring home knowledge.*

Samuel Johnson

Travel Records

Where Visited ....

....

Date of Departure ....

Date of Return ....

Who Went ....

....

....

....

....

....

Mode(s) of Transport	☐ Car	☐ Plane	☐ Boat
	☐ Train	☐ Other	

Accommodation	☐ Hotel	☐ B&B/ Guest Hs.	☐ With friends/ Self-catering
	☐ Camping/ Caravan	☐ Other	

Travel Records

Packing List

....

....

....

....

....

....

....

....

....

....

....

....

....

Travel Records

Packing List (cont.)

.... | ....
.... | ....
.... | ....
.... | ....
.... | ....
.... | ....

Check List (before leaving home)
e.g. turning off taps, locking doors & windows etc.

.... | ....
.... | ....
.... | ....
.... | ....
.... | ....

Travel Records

Expenses

Budget ....

Foreign Currency ....

Travellers Cheques (or similar) ....

| *Major Expenditure* | *Amount* | |
Item	Allocated	Spent
Travel		
Accommodation		
Dining Out		
Sight Seeing		
Souvenirs & Gifts		
Clothes		
First Aid		

Travel Records

Insurance Details

....

....

Travel Agent Details

....

Important Numbers

....

....

....

....

....

Notes

....

....

Travel Records

Diary

(using this format you can write as little or as much about each day as you like)

Date   Description

....

....

....

....

....

....

....

....

....

....

....

....

....

Travel Records

Diary

Date   Description

....

....

....

....

....

....

....

....

....

....

....

....

....

....

....

Travel Records

Diary

Date   Description

Travel Records

Diary

Date   Description

....

....

....

....

....

....

....

....

....

....

....

....

....

....

....

....

Diary

Date	Description
	....
	....
	....
	....
	....
	....
	....
	....
	....
	....
	....
	....
	....

Travel Records

Special Memories

Favourite Excursion:

....

....

....

....

....

....

Favourite Meal:

....

....

....

....

....

Travel Records

Special Memories (Cont.)

Favourite Place:

....

....

....

....

....

....

Notes:

....

....

....

....

....

Travel Records

Souvenirs

Item   Where Bought

....

....

....

....

Gifts

Item   For Whom

....

....

....

....

....

Travel Records

Trip 5

*A man's feet must be planted in his country,
but his eyes should survey the world.*

George Santayana

Travel Records

Where Visited ....
....

Date of Departure ....

Date of Return ....

Who Went ....

....

....

....

....

....

Mode(s) of Transport	☐ Car	☐ Plane	☐ Boat
	☐ Train	☐ Other	

Accommodation	☐ Hotel	☐ B&B/ Guest Hs.	☐ With friends/ Self-catering
	☐ Camping/ Caravan	☐ Other	

Travel Records

Packing List

....
....
....
....
....
....
....
....
....
....
....
....
....
....
....

Travel Records

Packing List (cont.)

....

....

....

....

....

Check List (before leaving home)
e.g. turning off taps, locking doors & windows etc.

....

....

....

....

....

Travel Records

Expenses

Budget ....

Foreign Currency ....

Travellers Cheques (or similar) ....

| Major Expenditure | Amount | |
Item	Allocated	Spent
Travel		
Accommodation		
Dining Out		
Sight Seeing		
Souvenirs & Gifts		
Clothes		
First Aid		

Travel Records

Insurance Details

....

....

Travel Agent Details

....

Important Numbers

....

....

....

....

....

Notes

....

....

....

Travel Records

Diary

(using this format you can write as little or as much about each day as you like)

Date   Description

....

....

....

....

....

....

....

....

....

....

....

....

....

....

....

....

Diary

Date   Description

....

....

....

....

....

....

....

....

....

....

....

....

....

Diary

Date	Description

Travel Records

Diary

Date   Description

....
....
....
....
....
....
....
....
....
....
....
....
....

Travel Records

Diary

Date   Description

....

....

....

....

....

....

....

....

....

....

....

....

....

Travel Records

Special Memories

Favourite Excursion:

....

....

....

....

....

....

....

Favourite Meal:

....

....

....

....

Travel Records

Special Memories (Cont.)

Favourite Place:

....

....

....

....

....

....

Notes:

....

....

....

....

....

Travel Records

Souvenirs

Item	Where Bought
....	....
....	....
....	....
....	....

Gifts

Item	For Whom
....	....
....	....
....	....
....	....
....	....

Travel Records

Trip 6

Things seen are mightier than things heard.

Alfred, Lord Tennyson

Travel Records

Where Visited ....

Date of Departure ....

Date of Return ....

Who Went ....

....

....

....

....

....

Mode(s) of Transport

☐ Car   ☐ Plane   ☐ Boat

☐ Train   ☐ Other

Accommodation

☐ Hotel   ☐ B&B/ Guest Hs.   ☐ With friends/ Self-catering

☐ Camping/ Caravan   ☐ Other ....

Travel Records

Packing List

Travel Records

Packing List (cont.)

....

....

....

....

....

....

Check List (before leaving home)
e.g. turning off taps, locking doors & windows etc.

....

....

....

....

....

Travel Records

Expenses

Budget ....

Foreign Currency ....

Travellers Cheques (or similar) ....

| *Major Expenditure* | *Amount* | |
Item	Allocated	Spent
Travel		
Accommodation		
Dining Out		
Sight Seeing		
Souvenirs & Gifts		
Clothes		
First Aid		

Travel Records

Insurance Details

....

....

Travel Agent Details

....

Important Numbers

....

....

....

....

Notes

....

....

Travel Records

Diary

(using this format you can write as little or as much about each day as you like)

Date   Description

....

....

....

....

....

....

....

....

....

....

....

....

Travel Records

Diary

Date   Description

....
....
....
....
....
....
....
....
....
....
....
....
....
....

Travel Records

Diary

Date   Description

....
....
....
....
....
....
....
....
....
....
....
....
....
....

Travel Records

Diary

Date   Description

....

....

....

....

....

....

....

....

....

....

....

....

— Travel Records —

Diary

Date	Description

....
....
....
....
....
....
....
....
....
....
....
....
....
....

Travel Records

Special Memories

Favourite Excursion:

....

....

....

....

....

....

Favourite Meal:

....

....

....

....

Travel Records

Special Memories (Cont.)

Favourite Place:

....

....

....

....

....

....

....

Notes:

....

....

....

....

....

Travel Records

Souvenirs

Item   Where Bought

....

....

....

....

....

Gifts

Item   For Whom

....

....

....

....

....

Names & Addresses

Travelling is a wonderful way of getting to know
people. Make a note of your new friends' addresses
to enable you to keep in touch.

Name: ....

Address: ....

....

....

Name: ....

Address: ....

....

....

Name: ....

Address: ....

....

....

I am a citizen of the world.

Diogenes the Cynic

Names & Addresses

Name: ....

Address: ....

....

....

Name: ....

Address: ....

....

....

Name: ....

Address: ....

....

....

*Travelling may be one of two things —
an experience we shall always remember,
or an experience which, alas, we shall never forget.*

Rabbi Julius Gordon

Names & Addresses

Name: ....
Address: ....

....

....

Name: ....
Address: ....

....

....

Name: ....
Address: ....

....

....

Never have I been able to settle in life.
Always seated askew, as if on the arm of a
chair; ready to get up, to leave.

André Gide

Names & Addresses

Name: ....

Address: ....

....

....

....

Name: ....

Address: ....

....

....

....

Name: ....

Address: ....

....

....

....

The world only exists in your eyes —
your conception of it. You can make it as
big or as small as you want to.

F. Scott Fitzgerald

Names & Addresses

Name: ....

Address: ....

....

....

Name: ....

Address: ....

....

....

Name: ....

Address: ....

....

....

Like all great travellers, I have seen more
than I remember, and remember more
than I have seen.

Benjamin Disraeli

Names & Addresses

Name: ....

Address: ....

....

....

....

Name: ....

Address: ....

....

....

....

Name: ....

Address: ....

....

....

The less a tourist knows, the fewer
mistakes he need make, for he will not
expect himself to explain ignorance.

Henry Adams

Names & Addresses

Name: ....

Address: ....

....

....

Name: ....

Address: ....

....

....

Name: ....

Address: ....

....

....

For my part, I travel not to go anywhere,
but to go. I travel for travel's sake.
The great affair is to move.

Robert Louis Stevenson

Names & Addresses

Name: ....

Address: ....

....

....

Name: ....

Address: ....

....

....

Name: ....

Address: ....

....

....

*The difference between landscape and
landscape is small, but there is a great
difference in the beholders.*

Ralph Waldo Emerson

Names & Addresses

Name: ....

Address: ....

....

....

Name: ....

Address: ....

....

....

Name: ....

Address: ....

....

....

*When you travel, remember that a foreign country is
not designed to make you comfortable. It is designed
to make its own people comfortable.*

Clifton Fadiman

Names & Addresses

Name: ....
Address: ....
....
....

Name: ....
Address: ....
....
....

Name: ....
Address: ....
....
....

*I have found out that there ain't no surer
way to find out whether you like people or
hate them than to travel with them.*

Mark Twain

Notes

Notes

Notes

Notes